Away From Home

by

Rob Ward & Martin Jameson

Published by Playdead Press 2014

© Rob Ward and Martin Jameson 2014

Rob Ward and Martin Jameson have asserted their rights under the Copyright, Design and Patents Act, 1988, to be identified as the authors of this work.

A CIP catalogue record for this book is available from the British Library.

ISBN 978-1-910067-07-9

Caution

All rights whatsoever in this play are reserved and application for performance should be sought through the authors, before rehearsals begin, to 42 M&P Ltd, 8 Flitcroft Street, London WC2H 8DL Tel: +44 (0)207 292 0554 Email: Madyneil@42mp.com. No performance may be given unless a license has been obtained.

This book is sold subject to the condition that it shall not by way of trade or otherwise, be lent, resold, hired out, or otherwise circulated without the publisher's prior consent in any form of binding or cover other than that in which it is published and without a similar condition including this condition being imposed on the subsequent purchaser.

Printed by BPUK

Playdead Press
www.playdeadpress.com

Away From Home was first performed on 19 July, 2013 at New Century House as part of the 24:7 Theatre Festival in Manchester. It was a Working Progress Theatre Company Production. The company was as follows:

KYLE   Rob Ward

Director   Martin Jameson
Producers   Rob Ward & JoJo Kirtley Pritchard
Design & Lighting   Martin Jameson
Sound Design   Owen Rafferty
Stage Manager   Liam Straw

This version of the script was revised for a spring tour, 2014, which premiered at the Library Theatre's RE:Play Festival at The Lowry Theatre Salford. It was first performed on 30th January 2014, and was a co-production between Working Progress Theatre Company and Hartshorn-Hook Productions. The Play was performed at the Jermyn Street Theatre, London, 11th – 28th March 2014. The company was as follows:

KYLE   Rob Ward

Director   Martin Jameson
Producers   Rob Ward, Brian Hook, Louis Hartshorn & JoJo Kirtley Pritchard
Design & Lighting   Martin Jameson
Sound Design   Owen Rafferty
Stage Manager   Gabi Herrett

The Creative Team

MARTIN JAMESON (Co-Writer, Director and Design) grew up in Essex and went on to study Drama at Manchester University in the late 1970s. He has been working in TV, radio and theatre for over three decades. After a short stint as an actor and musical director, Martin became Associate Director at Nottingham Playhouse and directed at theatres all around the country including The Young Vic, West Yorkshire Playhouse and York Theatre Royal. Several years producing Radio Drama and Features for the BBC followed, and then a long stint writing exclusively for broadcast media. TV writing includes **Holby City, Casualty, Emmerdale, The Bill, Children's Ward** – plus more radio drama than he can remember, including many episodes of the BBC Radio 4 favorite, *Stone*. Martin recently returned to theatre, directing **Better Times & Saturday Night & Sunday Morning** for The Arden Theatre School; **Hidden** for the RE:Play Festival at The Lowry Theatre in 2013 (also published by Playdead Press); and in 2012 helmed **Working Progress Theatre Company's** debut show, **Loaded.** Martin still lives in Manchester and has no intention of returning to Essex any time soon.

ROB WARD (Co-Writer, Producer, Actor & Evertonian) was born on The Wirral and studied English and Drama at The University of Manchester where he learned his craft with numerous adventures on the Edinburgh Fringe. Rob graduated in 2009 and has worked as a actor and writer ever since, establishing Working Progress Theatre Company along with Jo Kirtley-Pritchard in 2011. In its short life, the company has produced a series of striking and innovative projects including **Lamp Oil** (an inter-active Halloween chiller performed in the Eagle Inn in Salford); **Champion** (which Rob scripted) as part of 'To Russia With Love' a theatrical protest against homophobia at the Sochi Winter Olympics, at The Contact Theatre Manchester; the award winning **Loaded** by Jo Kirtley Pritchard, in which Rob played the part of Dillon; and the 'C' Project, raising money for Manchester's world renowned Christie Cancer Hospital.

Other acting credits include JB Shorts 10 (Real Life Theatre), Out/Loud (Hope Theatre), Asylum Of Grace (Dream Avenue), and George Harrison in Ticket To Write (Unity Theatre). Rob has appeared at the Royal Exchange as part of their Pub season, and toured Italy for four months in Robin Hood. As a writer Rob has also worked with Action Transport Theatre on Last Train Home as part of 'Four For The Port', and with Theatre By Numbers on the interactive dining piece Murder At The Theatre.

The Kitchen/Living Room of a small flat, somewhere in a large northern city. It's pretty low rent; a sofa, table, breakfast bar with kettle and vodka, tea bags and milk.

Darkness, apart from moonlight through a window. Night city traffic hums in the distance, the occasional siren passing, a dog barks far away...

As our eyes become accustomed to the darkness, we clock the story of last night. A half eaten Chinese takeaway on the table. Empty coffee cups – wine glasses – half full... an uncompleted spliff on the coffee table. Clearly they never got that far. There's a trail of clothing... Jeans, T-shirt... A pair of Calvin Kleins...

Kyle's jacket hangs on the back of a chair.

The silence is broken by the opening phrase of Match of the Day – on repeat, and rather loud. Kyle's ringtone. The phone – in Kyle's jeans – is also on vibrate, buzzing against the sofa.

After a few rings, bleary Kyle stumbles through from the bedroom. He's got a great body, but he walks with some discomfort. He is naked apart from a towel, draped vaguely for modesty, in case of unexpected flatmates. He doesn't switch on the light. Kyle gropes for his phone. Checks the number. Scowls. Answers.

Kyle: (HUSHED, TIGHT ANNOYANCE) How d'you get this number? .... How many times?! We're finished... Well

I'm finished. ... No, I don't want to listen to you. I'm not stupid. I know exactly what kind of money... (LISTENS – HIS EYES WIDEN) Really? But I'm still not interested... (HE'S WAVERING) ... I don't owe you anything. (LISTENS, SIGHS, WEARY, GIVING IN) Well... ok. When? Where?

The main light goes on with a click. KYLE starts. In the glare we can see that he has a variety of injuries, bruising, and operation scars in the process of healing. They look nasty.

(INTO PHONE) I'll call you back. (HE HANGS UP)

Kyle's bed companion has come into the room. Kyle is momentarily self conscious, covering himself properly, hurriedly putting on his clothes, slipping his Calvin Kleins on, jeans, T-shirt... It's painful trying to get dressed in a hurry.

Sorry. Didn't wanna wake you. (RE PHONE) Oh it was... (HE CAN'T BRING HIMSELF TO TELL THE TRUTH)... family. (BEAT – HE KNOWS HOW UNCONVINCING THAT WAS) Ok... it wasn't family. It was... an old friend. Work thing...

No. I'm not with anybody. (BEAT) No. It's not my girlfriend. No, I'm not married. Really? You think I'm married? (LAUGHS, BITTER, RUEFUL) Actually, no it's not odd... (RE THE PHONE CALL) ...coz I used to work nights. Look... I gotta split.

Yeah. Course I like you. (PAUSES) I like you a lot. But... it's not gonna work. I'm sorry. I mean that. I really am sorry... I'll call you. Maybe. (BEAT)

The phone rings again. Kyle answers, putting on his shoes.

(INTO PHONE) I said. I'll ring you back. (HANGS UP)

No. You don't wanna know. You really don't wanna know. Ok! (HE'S HEADING FOR THE DOOR) For fuck's sake! *I* don't want to tell *you*!! (IT'S CLEARLY PAINFUL FOR HIM)

The phone rings again.

(INTO PHONE) Vincent! I will ring you. I promise.

He hangs up, about to go. Considers. Weary.

Vincent. Fucking things up for me. (RELENTS) You know... you... and me... last night... none of it would've happened if it weren't for Vincent. Stupid cunt.

Kyle comes back into the room. As Kyle becomes drawn into trying to explain the situation, so he uses the stuff around the flat – props and furniture - to illustrate his story.

(DOUBTFUL) You... into football at all..? Ok, well, all *this*, (REFERRING TO PHONE) it all goes back to last August... in fact, I can tell you the exact day. First match of the season. I'm in the Catcher. Yeah. The Oyster Catcher. Where we were tonight. (AMUSED) Yeah. I could tell you weren't a regular. (REACTS TO SMELL) Can't be arsed with it in the summer. Beautiful game but fucking awful smell. Stale ale, fat bastards and yellow muzzies. All the regulars back from burning two weeks in Alicante. And to what?

Hope.

Maybe this year. The back four look solid, the left winger's world class and the new lad up front's been knocking them in for fun pre-season.

Three points today boys, no hassle. I swig me pint. Jonno's got his phone out trying to show McQueen a picture of some bird he's met on holiday in Abersoch. McQueen doesn't look up: 'Nice arse mate'

(AS JONNO) 'You din't even look!'

McQueen always knows how to wind Jonno up. (AS MCQUEEN) 'Nice tits.'

(JONNO) 'Oi! McQueen, you cunt, she's not just some tits and no brains like fucking stupid or nothing mate. She's, like, *re-taking* her first year at uni. She knows what she wants.'

I can't resist. 'And that's you, is it, Jonno?'

'Fuck off, Kyle, when was the last time you had a shag?'

Then my phone goes. My work phone. I used to have, like, a separate phone for that job I was telling you about.

Kyle picks a phone off the breakfast bar to demonstrate with. He checks it.

Vincent. The fucker knows I'm not working today.

But now Jonno's trying to grab the phone, coz he wants to see if it's a dirty text.

Kyle is holding the phone out of Jonno's reach.

(KYLE) 'It's me Uncle. Work.'

(JONNO) 'Tell him to fuck off.' Jonno don't like it when I duck out of a match day.

(KYLE) 'It's off, okay, phone's off.'

McQueen's rounding us up and we're heading for the turnstiles. Nearly miss the kick-off, thanks to Jonno pissing around at the burger van coz: 'they've got the wrong mustard!'.

Kyle's squeezing his way to his seat.

Get to our seats – (TO PUNTER) 'Sorry mate....' – and... bang – ball in from deep and the keeper's dropped it, scramble, go on, OH! Go on...! In your head you've seen that ball cross the line already, but not... quite... yet...

YES!!!!

Right on cue, Jonno's gone mental. Grabs my shoulder. 'Come onnnnnnn!' Burger goes flying. Never mind the wrong mustard. 'Sorry mate.'

Neat one-two on the edge, he's through, OOOOOOW! The crossbar. Fuck off, the crossbar! Jonno's practically crowd surfing.

And that sets the tone for the rest of the half. Crossbar, twice. Post, once. Off the line!

(KYLE TO MCQUEEN) 'The only thing keeping them in the game is their goalie'

(MCQUEEN) 'And this lot are meant to be challenging us for Europe?'

(KYLE) 'Fuck off!'

Start of the second half. The cockney bastards are making a change. Oh. It's *Him*.

(KYLE) 'Fucking hell, is he fit? I mean, he's quality, isn't he?'

(MCQUEEN) 'He's past 30 now.'

(KYLE) 'I dunno, Mac, he's top fucking class on his day.'

Jonno's not listening: 'You fat bastard! You fat bastard!'

Second half. We've taken the pressure right off. Forty-five minutes of my life I won't get back. Stadium announcement wakes us up: (AS P.A.) 'A minimum of four minutes added time.'

(JONNO TO REF) 'Where the fuck did that come from, nobhead?'

We're on our feet. Jonno squeezes my arm as they come forward one last time.

(JONNO) 'Just blow the fucking whistle ref…!'

Shit where's our full back gone?!? They're in down the right, ball sent over.

(GROANS) Would you fucking believe it?!!

And we're shuffling towards the exit. Victory snatched away from us with the last fucking kick.

And it was Him, wasn't it. You've seen Him do it before. Proving his value time and time again despite the growing number of grey hairs. Look at their Italian manager, kissing him on the cheek, licking his arse...

(JONNO) 'Fuck off ya daego twat!'

(MCQUEEN) 'Jonno mate, that's generally a term reserved for the Spanish.'

The Catcher. Post match pint.

That was when I did it. I still don't know why. I mean, like I say, it was my day off. But... we were all feeling like shit, not much of an atmosphere, so I thought: I'll just check.

Kyle checks his work phone.

Twelve missed calls. Three voicemails. I call him – tho' I'm not letting on that I give a shit.

Kyle heads somewhere private.

(ABRUPT) 'Vincent?'

(AS VINCENT ON THE PHONE) 'Kyle sweetheart, I know you're not supposed to be working.'

'No suppose about it Vincent, I'm not.'

'But you rang me back anyway.'

'To tell you to fuck off, Vincent.'

'Kyle, this isn't any old customer.'

'He can fuck off. I told you, I'm don't work Saturdays now the season's started.'

'Come on Kyle. A good friend of mine has got in touch on behalf of someone very, very important and specifically requested you.'

I try not to smile. 'Yeah, yeah, yeah, Vincent, like I give a toss.'

Then he tells me how much. 'Give me an hour.'

'Good boy. Go clean and be good.'

'I am good Vincent, fuck off.'

Kyle hangs up. Heads back into the bar.

'Shit, lads I'd better make tracks. Me Uncle.'

(MCQUEEN) 'It's Saturday night…?'

'He's got a job on. All-nighter. Shop fitting.'

(JONNO) 'You said you weren't working. You know what, lad, you're turning into a proper armchair fan.'

(KYLE) 'Double time, Jonno.'

(JONNO) 'Fair do's, lad, fair do's.'

Kyle enters the swanky hotel.

Fuck off hotel, fancy foyer. Sixth floor...

Kyle steps into the lift and presses the button.

Ding!

Steps out of the lift.

Looking for six oh.... There. Right in the little corner. Six-oh-five.

He takes a deep breath.

Quiet knock. Nothing. That's when the butterflies are at their worst. Coz when you hear movement you know there's no going back. Footsteps. The door opens.

No. Fucking. Way.

It's Him.

'Sorry mate, I was looking for 605, must be...'

He points to the number. 'Come in.'

Straight into the bedroom. He shuts the door.

(FOOTBALLER) 'So let's get it out the way. You know who I am, yeah?'

(KYLE) 'Never seen you before in my life, mate.' Face like a fucking cherub.

That gives him a new lease a life. He's unbuttoning his shirt so I take that as my cue. Should I say anything? He seems to know what he's doing.

Suddenly, Jonno's in my head. '*You fat bastard. You fat bastard.*' Not on this evidence mate.

'What..?' He's looking at me.

'Nothing.'

When He's stripped off He picks his wallet off the bedside table and makes the payment. He's watching me.

Kyle is unsettled. He tries to regain control as he takes his shoes off.

(KYLE – TO HIMSELF) 'Come on mate, I know its impressive but fucking professionalism yeah.'

When I turn back, his cock is in my face. There's a condom and lube in the second draw.

(FOOTBALLER) 'Fuck me.'

Fuck me! The fella whose goal robbed my team of two points today is bending over a bed asking me to fuck him. Me to fuck him.

So I do.

Slow at first. I don't know if this is his first time or what. He seems unsure. As I'm getting going, he lets out this whimper. I know straight away the difference between what's hot and what's sore.

(KYLE) 'You OK?' He looks me in the eyes.

(FOOTBALLER) 'Yes.' He didn't look it.

'Different position?'

'Thanks.'

It was... good.

After, when I get back from the bog, He gets me to lie there next to him for a bit. Holding me.

And in that moment, I just can't resist: 'You're a jammy cunt y'know. Where did them four extra minutes come from?'

Bad idea.

(FOOTBALLER - ANGRY) 'You said you didn't know who I was.'

'Alright mate, chill out.'

'Why d'you lie?'

'Come on, I'm winding you up.'

He looks at me like I've crapped in his mini bar.

(KYLE) 'I only said nowt coz I didn't wanna make you shit yourself more than you already probably were. I thought it was what you wanted to hear. Part of the service and all that. And anyway, you're the one who calls for me. I don't have a fucking clue who's behind that door.'

'Well, go on, then. Fuck off back out of it.'

'Gladly.'

Kyle grabs his T-shirt and heads back to the lift.

I'm in the lift and it stops on the second floor. This posh fortysomething bird in a fur coat gets in. Gives me a funny look. Must be that big fucking grin on my face.

The lift door opens.

Ding!

***

Sunday morning.

Kyle's phone vibrates. He stirs, but goes back to sleep again. It vibrates again. Kyle hauls himself up, and finds his phone.

One new voicemail - on the private phone.

He calls the voicemail. Listens.

(TO SELF) 'Oh fuck off mum…'

Listens to the rest of the message, closes his eyes and groans.

Mum and dad live across town. Far enough to get breathing space; not far enough to avoid invites to Sunday lunch.

(MUM) 'Kyle, love, I know you're busy…' She's got *that* tone in her voice. 'Your dad's got something he needs to say to you…'

He hangs up.

Dad runs his own business. Self made man, with the emphasis on the 'man'. Facilities Procurement or something. Sounds flash, but basically it's just shifting kit around. Me mum loves it coz she gets a plush pad in the leafy suburbs and coffee mornings with the other Stepford wives. They've known I'm gay for a couple of years now. But they don't talk about it. No. They *won't* talk about it. Which is why I'm always busy on a Sunday.

He opens the door before I can get the key in the lock. 'Half one your mother said. Your dinner's been sat on the table fifteen minutes'

'Hi dad, lovely to see you too. I'm fine, thanks for asking.'

Mum jumps in. 'Come through love. I've put it back in the oven. I'll make some more gravy'

'Mum, its fine…'

'You can't reheat gravy love.'

Kyle sits at the table where he and his unseen partner were eating the Chinese takeaway the night before.

Shiv – my kid sister – is texting under the table. Mum starts with the Mastermind routine. 'So how's work, love?'

My dad makes a noise through his food, which I take to be sarcastic.

(KYLE) 'Actually dad. It's turning out to be a good earner. I know what I'm doing.'

(DAD) 'Frittering your life away.'

(MUM) 'Alan, he's showing a bit of initiative. You of all people should respect that.'

(DAD) 'Well I might if I actually knew what it is he does.'

(KYLE) 'Ehm, hello. I am here.'

(DAD) 'So?'

(KYLE) 'I... basically sell things for other people on eBay.'

(DAD) 'And these people are too bone idle to turn on a computer and do it themselves?'

(POINTED) 'It's like you're always saying, Dad, we've turned into a nation of lazy arses.'

(MUM) 'Language.'

Shiv shrugs.

(DAD) 'It's hardly a viable business plan. It's a gimmick.'

(KYLE CHANGES THE SUBJECT) 'Sooo, Shiv, how's school?'

(DAD PICKS UP HIS KNIFE) 'I haven't finished.'

Mum puts a hand on his arm. 'Alan...' He shakes her off. 'Dad. I've got a roof over my head – and I pay for it myself.'

Mum glares at him. He re-groups. 'Kyle, I know you've needed some time to "do your own thing" but – how can I put it? – I worry about you, son.'

I want to tell him how big a pile of shite that sounds - but I just think about last night and smile.

(DAD) 'So, the reason your mum… that I asked you here is there's a post opening up at the business.'

(KYLE) 'Working with you?'

(DAD) 'It's a proper job.'

Mum's glaring at me now. Don't rise to it.

(TIGHT) 'I'll think about it dad'

'I'd like to have one of my own in place. I mean, I won't be around forever and…'

Shiv's zoned out texting. Mum's smiling tightly at me, willing me to say yes.

(KYLE) 'I've got my own business, Dad.'

(DAD) 'Selling junk on eBay.'

'There's a bit more to it than that.'

'Is there? What exactly? Where's the future in it? Eh? I'm offering you a future, son. Don't you want a future?'

Mum cuts in. 'Anyone for Tiramisu?'

I take the hint. 'Shiv? I was asking you about school.'

Mum answers for her. 'She's doing really well. Alayna's mum thinks it's between her and Kelsey for head girl.'

Dad waits for mum to take his plate. 'Be nice to have one of my kids make it to their A-levels.'

(KYLE TRIES TO CHANGE THE SUBJECT) 'D'you want some help mum?'

And then dad says it. 'And she's got a boyfriend.'

(KYLE) 'Oh yeah. Anyone I know?'

Dad answers for her. 'Yes, we were getting worried, weren't we, Val. I mean, one's enough for this family.'

And suddenly this huge elephant that has been sitting in the room for over two years gets up and takes an enormous shit over the dinner table.

(KYLE) 'And you wonder why I don't want to come and work with you.'

(DAD) 'I'm just being honest. Like you were with me.'

'Get used to it, Dad, because I'm happy.'

'No, son, you're not happy. You're my son, and I know you're not happy. Not being... what you are. You can't be.'

I want to hit him. But I've got a better idea.

(KYLE) 'You wanna know why I'm happy? Eh dad? Coz if you offer the right service, you can earn seventy, maybe eighty quid for half an hour's work.'

'What do you mean love?' Mum doesn't know where to look. Even Shiv stops texting.

'And that's why I don't wanna go into business with you, dad. I'd much rather be paid to have sex with men than have to listen to your endless shit.'

He looks at me. It's as good as a smack in the face, and I'm glad.

(KYLE) 'Well you wanted to know what I do – what I really do - so I'm telling you.'

Kyle storms out.

I don't look back til I get to the bus stop, double quick time, heart pounding. I check my phones. My hand's shaking. Nothing from work. Two missed calls on my personal phone. Don't recognize the number.

I return the call, watching an old, exhausted Asian lady, wondering what shit she's going through right now. Phone picks up.

It's Him. (FOOTBALLER) 'Finally.'

(KYLE HIDING HIS PANIC) 'How d'you get this number?'

(FOOTBALLER) 'I rang my phone from yours last night, when you were in the bathroom, after... y'know.'

I do my best to sound annoyed. 'Okay. And?'

'I've got a few hours before I head back to London.'

'And?' Bastard was gonna have to work for it.

'Only problem is, I've had to check out of the hotel.'

(DRY) 'Really.'

'Where are you?'

'Why d'you wanna know?'

But he's not playing. 'Where are you?!'

I text him the post code. The white Audi pulls up as promised next to the park over the road.

He smiles when I get in and I manage to mumble an 'alright'. He heads further out of town. Driving in silence. It's uncomfortable - but after all the noise at my Dad's... I'm glad of it.

And then he pulls up, on a track behind some trees. It's normally cash up front, but I know he's good for it, and anyway... there's something about the way he smiles at me.

I never smile when a sixty year old librarian wheezes as I go down on him. Especially when he's got a cock the size of a button mushroom. I've learned to switch off, go numb and throw in a fake groan every now and then.

But now I smile back, because, well, it's with Him.

He asks me if I'll wear something when I'm fucking him. Expecting a gimp mask I say: 'Sure. Why not?'

And then he gets it out. (DISGUST) The Rag.

Kyle picks up a white T-Shirt that has been lying on the sofa.

(KYLE) 'You want me to fucking wear that?'

(ASIDE - EXPLAINING) Ok. Right. So there's 'us'. And there's 'them'. The Scum. The Filth. Two teams divided by the same city. And the fucker's got *their* home shirt stuffed in his glove compartment! He's horny as fuck and he's begging me to throw it on.

(KYLE) 'That'll be another fifty, ta'.

He lays out five *twenties* on the dash. I look around to check - not if anyone can see us doing it - but if anyone can see me wearing this piece of shit. As soon as I come, I take it straight off, wipe his stomach and throw it out of the window. I climb out the car and take a massive piss all over it.

He's laughing when I climb back into the car. He's laughing... and I am too.

(DELIBERATE PAST TENSE) And then... we kissed. And smiled. And kissed again.

He sticks the radio on and pulls out a packet of cigs. I pretend to look shocked.

(FOOTBALLER) 'Don't tell the gaffer,'

And then he starts. It's like he's answering questions I haven't even asked him.

He tells me about his family in London. The youngest of five, all boys, builders, soldiers, plumbers, proper working men. And him – the footballer. His first club, his first goal - the first time he went in for a tackle with a player he fancied. His parents know he's gay, his agent know he's gay. And they're cool with it, or so they say. He's thought about coming out, but they've all given him the 'career suicide' line.

It's like something he wants me to understand - *needs* me to understand.

I look at the clock. It's late afternoon now. 'You're leaving it a bit late to head back, aren't you? I mean, you gotta be training first thing.'

'Yeah. Well. The gaffer knows I stayed up here.'

'Oh yeah?'

'I might be wearing that shirt a lot more often. Preferably not one you've pissed on... but still.'

Kyle clocks the T-Shirt, and then looks at the footballer.

(KYLE) 'Are you signing for them scumbags?'

'You should see what they're offering me. And lets face it, I've got a better chance of getting into Europe...'

'Alright, fuck off, it's not an interview with Sky Sports.'

'So I'll be up living up here, possibly as soon as next week. This… could be a regular thing. If you want.'

What does that count as? A pull? A date? A proposal? It's none of them, but it has the ring of all three. (WINDED) Suddenly I'm feeling… Well I don't know what I feel.

He's staring at me. 'So? What d'you think?'

'I'm thinking I'll have the rest of my cash. Ta.'

'What?'

'Sorry to rush. Gotta be somewhere.'

'Aren't you gonna answer my question?'

(SHRUGS, ANNOYED) 'I'll think about it.'

'Why d'you need to think about it?'

'Because this is my job.'

He's angry now. He reaches into his wallet pulls out a wad of notes - doesn't bother to count them - and throws them at me.

Kyle gets out of the car.

(KYLE) 'If you want me again, go through Vince.'

(FOOTBALLER) 'Look, I know the kind of people you normally "work" for, and to be honest…'

'It's money mate. Their money's as good as yours. Except now you play for the scum, I might charge double.'

He winds the window down, but I'm eaten up by that rage that hits you on the stands when an opposition player scores a goal and starts kissing the badge just to rub your face in it. 'If you want to book me again please remember that Saturday is my day off. I watch the footy and then I go out and get hammered. And when you ring him, remind Vince of that as well.'

Kyle storms off.

Off I go. Don't know where the bus stop is; don't know the area. But I know exactly what I'm heading away from.

***

It takes Kyle a few seconds to calm himself down.

The next week's pretty quiet. No call-outs. Not one. (SHRUGS) Happens sometimes. Anyway, it's the second Saturday of the season and our first away match. Lunchtime kick off. We're sat in the Catcher watching it on Mike's new 48 inch plasma. Jonno's new bird, the one from Abersoch, she's invited herself over for the weekend. Jonno swears he tried every excuse under the sun but she wouldn't drop it. Like a pitbull – with a baby.

Her name's Carolyn. She's a rugby girl and makes it clear to us that: 'Football's a poof's game.'

Kyle smiles wryly to himself.

First half's a non-event. Their full back tripping over the linesman is the most entertaining moment.

Personal phone starts vibrating. Mum.

'You not gonna get that?' McQueen looks concerned. I've told him about the bust up on Sunday… missing out my grand revelation, of course.

'Can't be arsed. It'll be the same bullshit as last time.'

Jonno joins in: 'Fucking shit man. So you're a bender. So fucking what.' Then McQueen: 'You'd have thought they'd be getting used to the idea. I mean it's been two years.'

I hate not being honest with Mac. When I came out - to mum and dad... well, I don't know how I'd have got through it without McQueen. But some things – like what I do... It's like... I just can't.

Carolyn pipes up: 'Well, I love the gays me.'

(KYLE) 'Cheers Carolyn.'

(CAROLYN) 'You ask Christopher, all my friends are gays.'

I hadn't heard Jonno called Christopher since year nine.

(JONNO) 'How am I supposed to know that?!?'

(CAROLYN) 'You spoke to Danny on Skype.'

(JONNO) 'For about thirty seconds.'

(CAROLYN) 'Come on Christopher, it's flipping obvious!'

Suddenly my attention is drawn to Mike's 48 incher. Breaking news. Confirmation that He *has* signed for The Scum. Raised eyebrows at the bar.

(MCQUEEN) 'I reckon that'll be a decent signing.'

I need a second to think. 'I'm going for a smoke.'

The beer garden's busy, but I find a corner. I check my phones. It's like a tic. Nothing.

(JUDGE) 'Hello you.'

A voice behind me. I recognise that voice. Like red wine and a cheeseboard.

I remember every shag. High court judge. Nothing special. Early sixties. I've been with him twice this year. First time was a tiny plate of seared scallops in a freezing cold restaurant, followed by a massage in his hotel room. Second time was everything else in his hotel room.

(KYLE) 'If you're after anything, ring Vince. But I don't work Saturdays.' I wasn't breaking that rule second week in a row for this prick.

(JUDGE) 'Oh come on, now we're here, I'm sure we can agree something to our mutual advantage.'

'I'm serious. Ring Vince. Excuse me, second half is about to kick off.'

'I spoke to Vince this week. He told me you were "off the books".'

Fucking what?!

(JUDGE) 'But here you are. Lucky coincidence hey. So will you come back for an hour?'

Or it's something like that. I'm striding past him into the car park.

Kyle speed dials.

'Vince it's Kyle. You gonna tell me why it's been so quiet this week?'

Vince doesn't bother playing dumb. It was Him. The arrogant little fucker had done it. Spoke to Vince that night. Offered him a massive payoff so He can have me to fuck or be fucked whenever He fucking wants.

And Vince took it - took it and didn't even fucking tell me.

(VINCE) 'He's probably gonna phone you today to go through everything. It's good money Kyle and what about those legs.'

'You can't just sell me off like a shitting prize cow!'

'Kyle, listen to me. You are my employEE. If, as your employER, I decide to end our agreement, I am well within my rights.'

'Yeah, well, what happens when I tell him to fuck off, Vince? He comes back to you and demands his money back

because I would rather fuck on broken glass than fuck him.'
There's a massive cheer inside the pub.

'You're cute, Kyle, but you're still new to this. I've got guys with way more experience, and, let's be honest, they're better at it than you. The cock sells Kyle, the face doesn't matter, love.'

Kyle hangs up – incandescent with anger and frustration.

So I ring Him. He's on speakerphone. The Scum are kicking off at three; he's driving to the ground to be unveiled at half time. Cunt.

(FOOTBALLER) 'I was gonna ring you.'

(KYLE) 'I hope them shit heads are giving you a decent signing on fee mate coz this is a big weekly income you've gotta replace. I'm good at my job.'

(FOOTBALLER LAUGHS) 'Vince didn't seem too fussed.'

'Go fuck yourself.'

'Kyle, can I get a word in? Please?'

Kyle clenches his jaw, getting his breath back.

'I'm listening.'

'Well, not now, I'm nearly at the ground.'

'You'll fit in well with them scumbags.'

'I should have told you first. Asked you. Again. Talked it through. Properly.'

'Too fucking right.'

'I s'pose... I wanted to make a point. I'm... I'm sorry. I was out of order.'

(KYLE - SOFTENING) 'Yeah, you were.'

(FOOTBALLER) 'So...?'

It's a reluctant climb down for Kyle.

(KYLE) 'Text me your digs. I'll come round later. Maybe we can... maybe we can sort something.'

(FOOTBALLER) 'Oh. I can't tonight. There's a new club opening in town. Carpe Diem. Heard of it?'

'Yeah. Everyone's heard of it.'

'It's international break next week and we're off tomorrow. A few of the lads are going down. Gotta show my face.'

'Only not with me.'

'They're paying me.'

'See, most people normally do it the other way round. Pay for drinks and not for sex.'

'This isn't easy Kyle. You need to understand...'

'No! You understand you arrogant prick. I am not your fucking slave.'

Hangs Up. Furious.

I head back into the pub. Your Honour's waiting to get served. I move in close. 'You ready to go?' He puts his wallet back into his coat pocket. He's keen.

(KYLE) 'Give me one minute.'

I wriggle my way back to our table.

(JONNO) 'Where the fuck were you? Mate, what a goal. We're one-nil up.'

(KYLE) 'I've gotta shoot.'

McQueen stares at me. 'You OK?'

(SHRUGS) 'My dad...'

He doesn't believe me, and I hate myself for it.

Ten minutes later I'm fucking Your Honour up against the trouser press in his hotel room. Or at least I'm trying to, only… it isn't happening. I'm not even close – and I'm going soft. Because… I don't need to. Because guess who I can't get out of my head? Him. Fucking Him.

Him, with his shaved eyebrow and stupid fucking hair. And the way the muscle twitches under his tattoo when he…

Kyle stops himself.

I look down at this bald pig moaning and wriggling and I know I don't want to be doing this. I'm buttoning up my fly.

(JUDGE) 'What's going on?'

(KYLE) 'We're finished.'

'I paid for an hour.'

I pull the six twenties out my back pocket. 'Refund.'

Back on the street I check my phone. Another couple of texts from my mum but nothing important.

It's twenty past three. The Scum haven't signed him in time to play today so he'll be sat on his arse on a plush seat in the executive box, with the fans around him shouting 'get up you poof' when a player goes down easy. But, hey, plush seats...

A call from McQueen brings me round. 'How's it going?' I mumble something vague.

(MCQUEEN) 'Good result, wasn't it?'

(KYLE) 'Yeah. Fucking good one.'

'Can you get away? Tonight?'

'Yeah. Definitely.'

'Excellent. Jonno's brother's got us tickets for that club that's opening near the Ibis. You know?'

Didn't it just have to be. 'Carpe Diem?'

'Yeah that's the one. Fancy it?'

You know what, why the fuck not?

(MCQUEEN) 'Excellent.'

This could go either way. But I've been a bit shit on McQueen and Jonno recently. And it'll be fun seeing His face when I show up. Yeah. This'll be a laugh this. The risk is quite hot, too.

I neck four desperados before McQueen picks me up. It's your typical fancy new club, looks like every other fancy club and charges the same as every fancy new club. Shitheads in suits. Slags in skirts. Exactly the kind of place where you'd expect to see a footballer in VIP.

Kyle's getting gradually, aggressively drunk. He pours himself a vodka.

I'm enjoying myself. Taking the piss out of Jonno. Chatting shit with McQueen. One of Mac's accumulators has come through so there's shots between rounds. 'Cheers, Mac!'

Carolyn's in my ear. (CAROLYN SHOUTS AGAINST THE NOISE) 'I love Christopher, you know!'

(KYLE – *shouting back*) 'I can tell. I'm sure he feels the same.'

'D'you reckon?'

'Oh yeah. He's thinking of popping the question.'

(CAROLYN – *she can't hear above the noise*) 'What?'

(KYLE) 'Popping the question!'

'What???'

'He's going to ask you to marry him!!!'

'Christ on a fucking pedalo! I hope he does it somewhere proper romantic. You know my sister's fella?'

(KYLE) 'Oh yeah?'

'He proposed to her outside the Laser Quest in Colwyn Bay. She said she'd never forget it for as long as she lived.'

Then I see Him. He's with three of them I recognise. The Scum. With their girlfriends...

But, hang on a minute... Wait. Wait, wait... There's four of them. Four girlfriends. Three tossers. And a gay footballer.

My gay footballer. My – what? – fella? Boyfriend? Master?

What the fuck is it? ... (HARD) And who the fuck is that with him?

Some blond skank. Laughing at his jokes. He's not even funny.

(KYLE) 'McQueen. See them Scum over there?'

Kyle's losing it. Confused.

'Fucking scum. Scum! Hey Jonno. Jonno. Wanna go give them some shit?' I set off for VIP. Jonno's behind me.

Begins to chant

'WHO ARE YA? WHO ARE YA? WHO ARE YA?'

Every cunt in there turns and they're looking at me. And His face is like froze; like he's well bricking it.

'WHO ARE YA?'

Some big black fella comes over. Says something…

(KYLE – SHAKING HIM OFF) 'Yeah, alright mate.'

Jonno isn't singing. Fucking wuss. But I am. Louder - and louder. And it's not about The Scum. It's not about Vince; it's not about Your Honour; it's not about Mum and Dad. It's about Him.

I'm looking Him in the eye. Right in his lying little eye. And I'm belting them out. All the chants. 'Who are ya'? Who are ya'? Who are ya'?!'

And then the black fella comes back over, puts an arm on me. (AS KYLE) 'Fuck off mate.'

McQueen's pulling me over here. Then another fella's pulling me back over here. A table of drinks goes flying.

Kyle kicks the coffee table over.

Nasty nasty nasty smash....! Next thing, the pavement comes up to twat me in the face.

Kyle crashes to the ground.

I think that's McQueen, holding them off, coz they wanna stick the boot in. Top lad, McQueen. And then I puke everywhere.

McQueen drags me into a side alley. I can feel my lip and my left eye starting to swell. The taste of blood and regurgitated tequila...

Mac's using the elbow of his shirt to try and clean worst off.

(KYLE) 'Fuck off...'

(MCQUEEN) 'No, you fuck off.'

'No, you fuck off Mac. Jonno'll be waiting. I'll be fine. Fuck off. Fuck off!'

'Not til you tell me what the fuck's going on?'

Right on cue – bang! – a door in the alley crashes open. It's Him. Face likes he's on a hat-trick and just been subbed: 'What the fuck is going on?!'

(KYLE) 'No, I think I'm the one who gets to ask what the fuck's going on?'

'I saw you on the CCTV. I told them you were an old mate. You've got about two minutes to get your arse out of here.'

It takes a lot to shock McQueen, but judging by the location of his dropped jaw, Mac's pretty bloody gobsmacked: 'Excuse me? As regards to "what the fuck is going on?" I think I asked first.'

(FOOTBALLER) 'Who's this?'

(KYLE) 'McQueen. He's a mate. Mac, this is…'

(MCQUEEN) 'Yeah, Kyle. I know who this is. 'Tho' I'm so used to seeing him rolling around on the deck I nearly didn't recognize him stood up.'

(FOOTBALLER) 'Can we trust him?'

(KYLE - BITTER) 'We?'

(FOOTBALLER - SPELLING IT OUT) 'Can we trust him?!'

(KYLE) 'Always.'

He pulls out a key. 'It's for my new gaff.' He's scribbled the address on a beermat. (TO McQUEEN) 'Can you get him there? Make sure he's ok.'

Mac looks at Him and then at me. 'Is this what I think it is?'

(KYLE) 'It's a business arrangement.'

(MCQUEEN) 'What?!?'

Kyle can't hide his sense of shame – even though consciously he has no problem with it – it's about telling his mate and fearing the response, fearing that he'll lose the respect of his friend.

(SLOW, WARY) 'I don't fit shops for my uncle.'

I can see the cogs whirring in McQueen's head. I'm half expecting him to walk away. But he doesn't.

(MCQUEEN) 'Well, I s'pose I should be surprised... but then you always were shit at woodwork. Fuck me. My mate Kyle, the WAG.' He looks me in the eye. 'You sure you know what you're doing?'

(FOOTBALLER) 'Look, Mac, Kyle says you're ok, but this is between him and me, yeah?'

'I don't wanna see my best friend getting hurt. And I don't remember saying you could call me Mac.'

'He won't get hurt.'

'Well I think he was pretty bloody hurt tonight, don't you? I mean, who was that blond bit on your arm then.'

'Like he said, it's a business arrangement.'

(MCQUEEN – SARCASTIC, HARD) 'Oh, oh! That's ok then!' Mac's fired up, and suddenly I'm wondering why I ever doubted that I could tell him.

(FOOTBALLER) 'Ok! Ok all right! I should have told him about her.'

(MCQUEEN) 'Well he's here now, so tell him.'

He pulls me out of range of the CCTV. (FOOTBALLER – SOTTO) 'My agent knows someone who knows these girls. Socialites. Looks good for them to be seen out with me…'

I know bullshit when I hear it. 'You mean, for you to be seen out with them.'

He opens his mouth, but he knows he can't come up with anything good.

(KYLE) 'You know what? Forget it.'

Kyle storms off.

(FOOTBALLER) 'No! Kyle, stop. Listen to me, please. What happened to the last footballer in this country who came out? I mean, one who was actually still playing. He ended up hanging from the fucking roof of a Shoreditch lock-up!'

(KYLE CHANTS QUIETLY) 'Who are ya', who are ya'…'

'I could ask the same of you!'

'Go on then. Say it. Rent boy? Whore?'

'I didn't have you down as someone who was gonna go all gay rights on me.'

'This isn't about gay rights. This is about self respect.'

'Exactly. And when I met you I saw a guy who wanted out but was too proud to admit that. But I can help you. I want to help you - to get out.'

'That's not your call!'

'I'm saying, that I understand that this is your job, but I'm serious about you, you won't have to worry about money. I mean that. You'll have everything you need and more.'

'You think you can buy me – so you can treat me like shit.'

'How else am I gonna be able to see you and guarantee you aren't fucking other guys at the same time?'

'You could just ask me out.'

***

The Saturday before Christmas.

Kyle clears up the mess from the club, and flicks the kettle on.

I make myself a cappuccino with my new coffee machine – Lavazza – a hundred and seventy nine nicker! - and stick *Football Focus* on my 52 inch wall hung LED 3D HDTV. Way down below me the city is stirring to life. First Christmas in my new place. Let's just say it's got a great view.

No more pokey flats with door handles that pull off in your hand.

And yeah, I guess I'd like him to move in. But he lives in the same apartments as two of his team mates and he'd need to come up with a good reason to move away. I'm not gonna put that pressure on him.

He's still playing for The Scum. Just. Everyone knows he's most effective through the middle, any tosser'll tell you that, 'cept the manager has stuck him out on the right. So The Filth are down in mid table and it's funny as fuck.

Life is good. Football is good. Relationship is fucking great.

McQueen don't say owt, but I know what he thinks. I know he doesn't trust him.

Anyway, we've proved him wrong. We're not out on the streets hand in hand, but get real, it's not Amsterdam. If we have a night out, I'm his mate. If we go for dinner, I'm his brother.

Ok. We haven't actually been for dinner. But if we do, that's what we've decided.

(THOUGHTFUL) He's playing in London Boxing Day so he'll go down there for Christmas Day; see his family.

I'm having Christmas here (INDICATES THE ROOM HE IS IN) I've spoke to Mum once since the summer. I hung up on her. My dad hasn't bothered and neither have I. Yes, I miss them. I miss Mum. I'll miss her turkey. And her gravy.

After He gets off training, He comes and picks me up. We go for a drive. He doesn't get recognized thanks to shades and a beanie. Even if they do make him look like a complete twat.

He says he's got me something really cool for Christmas, but I can't think what it is, coz he's given me everything I could ever want already. I mean, he's already bought me a car. A fucking car. He paid cash! Second hand, like, but it's a Mazda MX5. One of those that gives Clarkson a stiffy. I don't think I've ever been this happy in my whole life.

Kyle's face falls.

It's getting dark when we get back to mine, but I've always had good eyesight.

(KYLE) 'Pull over.'

(FOOTBALLER) 'What?'

'I said, fucking pull over!'

It's Mum, at the gate, peering at the flat numbers.

(KYLE) 'She hasn't seen us. I'll walk the rest of the way.'

He's staring at me. Accusing. Hurt. 'Ring me when you're done.'

As he drives away, she's doing that thing where you look vaguely up at a building and assume the person inside will get that you're there.

She turns. It takes a second for it to register and then she runs towards me and throws her arms around me. She's crying. I hug her back. She smells of Christmas and home and I hug her a bit harder.

Into the apartment. Shit!

Kyle hides the spliff as he shows mum into the flat.

'Come through mum.'

(MUM) 'It's nice. It's nice, Kyle.'

I can tell she's a bit gob-smacked at the flat, the view and everything. But it's genuine. She wipes away another tear.

He starts making a cup of tea for mum.

(KYLE) 'How did you find me?'

'McQueen told me. He's worried as well.'

'McQueen? What? Did he come to one of your coffee mornings?'

'He says he hasn't seen a lot of you this last couple of months.'

'What else has he told you?'

'He's a good friend, Kyle.'

'Look Mum, why are you here?'

(MUM'S STILL UPSET) 'It's been four months Kyle. I've rung and I've text.'

Kyle takes her the cup of tea.

'Modern families mum. Some parents don't see their kids for years.'

'Not us Kyle. Not this family. I've been worried sick about you.'

'You've not exactly made it easy for me, mum.'

'I find this lifestyle choice of yours difficult.'

'What choice?'

'To sell yourself, Kyle. To sell yourself for sex.'

He starts to show her the door.

'Well, like you say, it's my choice. So… if that's everything…?!'

'About your Dad…'

'Sod Dad. Unless he's gonna come here and say sorry he can sod off and…'

'And what? And what Kyle?'

She's not angry. I want her to be angry, but she's not. And in that moment, I 'know'.

Sixty year old man. Fond of a pint. Cigar smoker. Hasn't broken sweat in twenty years.

Pause.

(KYLE) 'How long's he known?'

'Six months.'

Fuck. The fuckers hadn't told me. But then I hadn't given a shit about either of them for two years.

(MUM) 'He's taking time off work. I've made him. Money's a bit tight, what with Christmas coming up. We'll get by.'

When he opens the door he nearly hugs me.

(DAD) 'If it's not the worms in the office that'll get me, it's the ones in my arse.' You know, before all this shit between us, he used to joke all the time.

We talk. Not return of the prodigal son. But talk. Proper talk. 'Look dad. I hope you don't mind me saying. Mum mentioned about the money situation.'

'Nothing a couple of trips to the bookies won't sort.'

'With your luck? Dad. Let me help. I've got money. Have it. Please take it. One less thing to worry about during your treatment, yeah?'

'Well, you could always come and work with me, son. Like I said.'

(BEAT) 'No. No, dad, I'm sorry. The money I have is yours. But no, I can't work with you…'

'Why not?'

'It's not for me dad.'

'But *that* is?! I don't want your money son. I don't want a penny of it, because I know where it's come from and it's fucking disgusting. I don't want your money. I want a son I can be proud of.'

Kyle is overwhelmed and moves away. For a moment it seems he won't be able to continue with the story.

I've never heard him swear before.

Kyle leaps into his car.

I ring Him.

(FOOTBALLER) 'Hey, you OK?'

(KYLE - UPSET) 'Where are you?'

'Kyle? What happened?'

'I need to see you. I need to see you now.'

'In town. Just leaving my agent's flat.'

'You walking?'

'Yeah. Kyle? Is this about your mum?'

'I'm picking you up, wait there.'

He's waiting under the bridge just round the corner from his agent's. He gets in. He's wearing slim chinos. Ralph Lauren gilet. His hair looks good. He looks good. He always looks fucking good. Hot guy wants sex, I'm gonna say yes. Premiership footballer wants discrete sex. Sneaking around; fear of getting caught. Fucking horny. Yes. Magazines linking him with this model and that model and he's having sex with me.

He's telling me to calm down, but I am so up for it. Coz if all that with my dad's taught me one thing, it's that it's not about the money, or the independence - it's about the sex. And I want it. I really want it. And I'm good at it. And I love the look in a guy's eye when he's getting it and he knows it's good. That really, *really* turns me on.

I'm driving us out of town. Back to where we fucked behind those trees and I want to fuck him more than ever, and I want to fuck him now.

Why even wait?

I reach over and grab at his belt. Got it in one. He's pushing me away. The more he fights, the hornier I get.

(FOOTBALLER) 'Stop the car!'

But I put my foot down. Hand down his chinos. Feel it. He wrenches me away, fucking furious. Like a fucking fighting dog foaming and gnarling, all frantic hand movements...

And then the wheel catches the kerb – or something stupid – and we're upside down.

And everything's really slow - even his airbag exploding. Like in one of them documentaries.

And it's still. Just hot metal, ticking.

My airbag doesn't fire. I can't move. I think I'm in agonizing pain. But I'm not sure.

He's out of the car. He's crouching down, talking through the shattered window.

(FOOTBALLER) 'I've called an ambulance. You're gonna be all right.'

I'm not convinced. I can't feel anything, so I know it's bad. I say his name.

I can hear a siren in the distance.

'Kyle...'

'Wha..?'

'Kyle, can you hear me? Listen to me. I have to go.'

'Nooo!'

'You know the deal. I... I can't be here. You know the deal.'

All I could see was his feet as he ran off down the road. And then I passed out.

***

The lights change. Dramatic. A heart monitor beeps. Music underscores.

Guess whose face I see when I finally open my eyes?

McQueen. Big broken nose – and big brown eyes that fucking know everything.

(CROAKS) 'Oh bollox,' My throat feels like Gandhi's flip flop. 'I've died and gone to hell.'

He puts a finger on my lips. 'Shh. Doctor's here.'

The door swings open, and in walks this medic, in his scrubs, like in a shit episode of Holby City. Mask over his face. It's gonna be bad news. I shut my eyes.

But then... I can smell him. I know his smell. I open them again. I'm squinting against the light. I reach up and pull at the mask. I can't believe it. I can't stop the tears from flowing.

McQueen's watching from across the side ward: 'We had to smuggle him in. You wouldn't believe how hard it was to get those scrubs. I've promised to take this nurse on a date, and to be honest, she's a right dog. Don't ever say I don't do anything for you.'

But I'm not listening, because He's here. He's come back. He kisses me – very, very gently – and strokes my hair. Tells me about this goal He scored on Boxing Day.

Then McQueen says he's got another surprise for me. The door again, and another voice:

(DAD) 'Welcome back, son.'

Dad...?

For a moment, I'm awkward, being in the same room with my boyfriend - my lover - stroking my hair, and my Dad watching on, not even blinking: 'We've had a little chat. Me and him.' Dad takes my hand. 'I only want you to be happy, son.'

Then McQueen reaches into the cabinet next to my bed, pulls out a football. They're doing keepy-ups on the ward! They nearly smash one of those expensive respirator things. McQueen was always shit.

And I'm laughing. He's laughing. My dad's laughing too.

Pause.

Of course, all of that...

With a loud vinyl scratch, the music and heart monitor are gone. Lights snap back to normal.

…it's a load of bollox. You wanna know what really happened?

I open my eyes and I see McQueen. There's only one thing I want to know.

(CROAKY) 'Is he here? Has he been?'

(MCQUEEN) 'I was gonna give it a few days…'

McQueen picks up a paper that has been lying on the coffee table.

(MCQUEEN) 'Head butted our keeper at the derby. Straight red card. Six match ban. Jonno reckons he did it deliberately. Get himself suspended. Feet up at Christmas - then fuck off in January. There's talk of France, maybe Italy.'

'Can you go to him Mac? You know where he lives.'

'And say what, Kyle?'

Then Mum bursts in with two plastic coffee cups. 'So you're back with us, then?' She kisses me on the head and hands a cup to McQueen. I stare at Mac, and he makes his excuses. He knows. Mac always knows.

Mum strokes my hair: 'Your dad'll be in tonight.'

And sure enough, he is.

(DAD) 'If we'd lost you, Kyle. I'd've blamed myself. I would. Everyday for the rest of my life, I'd have blamed myself.'

(KYLE CROAKS) 'Good.'

'You can understand why I said what I did.'

'Don't you get it, Dad? You've lost the position in my life where what you say counts for anything.'

'Well. It's over now, anyway. All that. I mean, they're not here now, are they, your 'clients'?'

My heart's pounding. I can't speak. I hate the truth of it.

(DAD) 'All I want is for you to be happy. I'm sorry if that hasn't always shown like I meant it to. You're my son, and… you're my son, and I love you.'

(KYLE) 'So it's taken a near fatal car crash to say that. Fuck. Off. Dad.' I've never said those words to his face before. 'I don't know what to say Dad. I'm sorry I'm not the ideal son. I'm sorry you're ashamed of me…'

'I have never been ashamed of you Kyle!'

'Yes, you are!'

'I'm worried, confused…!'

'No, Dad, I really can't be arsed with it anymore.'

My dad's a tough man. In his eyes you can see a history. He's got rough cut features, all creases and hairs. He wants to say something. He wants the last word…

…but he leaves shortly afterwards.

It was January 3rd, he said.

(PAST TENSE) Christmas had come and gone.

They moved me onto the main ward.

McQueen popped in: 'I rang the buzzer and I kept ringing until a very angry Bulgarian lady answered and told me to piss off. The Scum are getting rid. He flew into Milan last night.'

(KYLE) 'Milan? In his Nike Air Max?'

McQueen smiled a proper warm smile. I looked at him. It was no good.

(KYLE) 'Prick.'

Mac shrugged.

(KYLE) 'Fucking prick. Fucking wanker fucking prick.' McQueen put a hand on my shoulder. 'You can say it if you want, Mac. Go on, say it. Say "I told you so."'

(MCQUEEN) 'No mate, it was only because of the stuff we hear on the terraces week in, week out. How does it go? "We won't give a fuck, when you're hanging from a tree, Judas cunt with HIV"; And where have they sent the World Cup to, mate? Russia, and fucking Qatar. The biggest two fingers Fifa could stick up. When I met him that night in the alley, I knew he didn't have the balls to stand up to that kind of shit.'

I wanted to tell him he was wrong, but I couldn't. Mac had to go. He called back from the end of the ward: 'Next time, mate, don't pick one of The Scum.'

***

Two weeks into the New Year I'm out. My mum has set up the spare room. Me and dad are exchanging grunts. He's not well. Shiv just goes on texting.

Jonno and McQueen are heading down the Catcher. I haven't watched any footie for a month. Turns out we're back in fourth place.

(JONNO) 'Ere are mate, cripple coming through.'

(KYLE) 'Say that again Jonno and you'll be fucking joining me.'

(JONNO) 'Alright lad, wind yer knob in.'

'Sorry, Jonno, I'm in a bit of a funny mood tonight.'

(MCQUEEN) 'Well if you want cheering up, why don't you ask Jonno what happened with Sweet Carolyn?'

(JONNO) 'Ey McQueen, I told you, I jibbed *her* off!'

(MCQUEEN) 'She dumped him. Apparently, he's not much of a conversationalist.'

(JONNO) 'Fuck off, McQueen, you blurt!'

Your Honour isn't in tonight, thank fuck. But he can't be the only one making a sneaky call behind the wife's back.

I'd always have a job. If I want it, it's there. That's what is so fucking difficult. Sat here, looking at rows and rows of potential clients. (CLOCKING SOMEONE) You'd be a kiss and a cuddle; (SOMEONE ELSE) you'd be dinner and a massage; (AND ANOTHER) and you'd just be a right dirty fuck.

I could call Vince now. He'll be expecting it. Coz I miss it. The fucking. But I know that if I do, it'll only lead back to Him. Or someone like him.

And then someone says my name. 'Kyle, yeah?'

I look round. And it's You.

A dog barks in the distance.

First thing you do is ask me how I got all this.

Kyle indicates his injuries.

I should have said: 'Nearly fucking killed in a car crash whilst wanking off a premiership footballer'. But I didn't and I was bull-shitting you the whole night, thinking it could be some kind of new start. And then, well, when Vince rang... I didn't want to lie to you, that's all. But... but I was afraid of telling you the truth too.

Kyle listens.

What do you mean, 'you haven't been telling me the truth either'?

He listens again, struggling to compute.

Say that again? You're on that college day release thing... with McQueen...? No, no, no, I introduced you. At the bar, he practically blanked you. (BEAT) He rang you? The little fucker. He set us up. (AFFECTIONATE) What a cunt.

The phone rings again. Match of the Day. Kyle looks at it.

Vince. Again.

He stares at Josh. At us.

Let it ring.

Slow fade to black.

The End.

```
@PJL COMMENT %%DocumentMedia: (A3) 842 1191 80 (white) (pl
@PJL COMMENT %KDKMedia: (A3) sides(2)
@PJL COMMENT %KDKEngineGRET: off
@PJL COMMENT %KDKSpool: on
@PJL COMMENT %KDKReqPunch: 0
@PJL COMMENT %KDKReqReorderSheets: facedown
@PJL COMMENT %%EndKPDComments
@PJL COMMENT %KDKSource: remove file:/var/spool/kodak_resou
@PJL COMMENT Kodak Digimaster 3 PCL 8.0 12.80
@PJL JOB NAME="BPUK19331_Insides_4upA3.pdf"
@PJL SET RESOLUTION=600
@PJL COMMENT %%Driver Build: 09.00.0005
@PJL COMMENT %%StartKPDComments
@PJL COMMENT %EK-JSE-3-0-Build: 08.01.0004
@PJL COMMENT %KDKBody: (A3) on
@PJL COMMENT %KDKPrintMethod: print
@PJL COMMENT %KDKOutputMedia:  stacker
@PJL COMMENT %%Requirements:  numcopies(1) staple(none)  fo
@PJL COMMENT %KDKRequirements: numcopies(1) staple(none)  f
@PJL COMMENT %KDKProofSet: 5 print
@PJL COMMENT %KDKCovers: (A3) none
@PJL COMMENT %KDKRotation: 0
@PJL COMMENT %KDKError: on (A3)
@PJL COMMENT %KDKActOn:
@PJL COMMENT %%Title: (BPUK19331_Insides_4upA3.pdf)
@PJL COMMENT %%For: (oce)
@PJL COMMENT %%Emulation: pcl5
@PJL COMMENT %%Routing: ()
@PJL COMMENT %%DocumentPrinterRequired: () (DS9110)
@PJL COMMENT %%DocumentMedia: (A3) 842 1191 80 (white) (pla
@PJL COMMENT %KDKMedia: (A3) sides(2)
@PJL COMMENT %KDKEngineGRET: off
@PJL COMMENT %KDKSpool: on
@PJL COMMENT %KDKReqPunch: 0
@PJL COMMENT %KDKReqReorderSheets: facedown
@PJL COMMENT %%EndKPDComments
```